OUT OF SPEECH

OUT OF

SPEECH

poems

ADAM VINES

Dear Peggy —
You are a
fine poet and brought such
insight and energy to the
Workshop. Thank you
for teaching me.

LOUISIANA STATE UNIVERSITY PRESS   BATON ROUGE

Published with the assistance of the Sea Cliff Fund

Published by Louisiana State University Press
Copyright © 2018 by Adam Vines
All rights reserved
Manufactured in the United States of America
LSU Press Paperback Original
FIRST PRINTING

DESIGNER: Barbara Neely Bourgoyne
TYPEFACE: Adobe Caslon Pro
PRINTER AND BINDER: LSI

Library of Congress Cataloging-in-Publication Data
Names: Vines, Adam, author.
Title: Out of speech : poems / Adam Vines.
Description: Baton Rouge : Louisiana State University Press, [2018]
Identifiers: LCCN 2017037426| ISBN 978-0-8071-6765-6 (pbk. : alk. paper) |
   ISBN 978-0-8071-6766-3 (pdf) | ISBN 978-0-8071-6767-0 (epub)
Classification: LCC PS3622.I55 A6 2018 | DDC 811/.6—dc23
LC record available at https://lccn.loc.gov/2017037426

For Grandmother and Great Aunt Marge,
who introduced me to art

CONTENTS

ACKNOWLEDGMENTS

I would like to thank Bob Hass and Eric Smith for their gracious and thoughtful suggestions for the poems and Dean Palazzo, Associate Dean Schnormeier, Alison Chapman, Peter Bellis, and the Alabama State Council on the Arts for providing support through grants and fellowships for my research and writing at museums. I would also like to thank Mary, Melissa, Mom, and my Sewanee family for their constant encouragement and love and Neal Novak and MaryKatherine Callaway for their keen eyes and ears and for helping so much in bringing this critter to bear.

I am thankful for the journals where these poems first appeared. Some of these poems appeared under different titles and ruminations:

"Not-Story" and "What Is Not Flesh Comes to a Point" in *Fogged Clarity*; "Borders" and "My View from Here" in *Tupelo Quarterly*; "The Apostle," "Tristesse I: Mattress as Canvas," "Tristesse II: Manifest Destiny, Late 20th Century," "Cortical Arousal," and "Re Stroke II" in *4ink7*; "Back to the Old City" and "*Muliercula:* Homunculus as Daughter," in *The Hopkins Review*; "Re-Stroke I" and "Theodicy" in *Green Mountains Review*; "Astrail Image as Ensign" in *The Greensboro Review.* "Four Moves to the Focal Point" in *Subtropics*; "Having Bummed a Smoke Outside of the National Gallery, Though I Have Quit," "A Study of Intergroup Reconciliation," "The Bluff," "The Kiss," and "Overheard," in *Ducts*; "Sentence" in *Waccamaw*; "Fisting the Tine" in *Sewanee Theological Review*; "Re-Stroke III: Still Life with Banyan Tree," "Memory as Burnt Fabric," and "Traymore Hotel: A Study in False Consciousness," in *Town Creek Review*; "Holes and Folds" in *The Journal*; "Blind Spot" in *Gulf Coast*; "When Pubic Becomes Public" in *72 Poems*; "On the Hay Ledge" in *Aura*; "The Philosophy of Subtraction" in *Five Points*; "Social Capital and the Introduction of the Vanilla Egg" and "Antipositivism" in *Connotation Press: an Online Artifact*; "When Pubic Becomes Public" and "Blind Spot" were reprinted in *Language Lessons,* published by Third Man Books, 2014.

OUT OF SPEECH

THE PHILOSOPHY OF SUBTRACTION

—Hopper's *Excursion into Philosophy*

Beds in everything today,
my borrowed one
back at the Marriott,

comforter bunched
at the foot, my dress socks
slung into folds

like half-dressed game.
It seems to be snowing
everywhere but here

and in Birmingham,
where my wife and daughter
are home early from school—

despite no accumulation—
both at the kitchen table, I'm sure,
my daughter's soup getting cold

while she drills her dolls
on subtraction, my wife
lassoing poor conjugations,

slashing *l'accent grave et aigu,*
the crockpot squatting
behind them, breaking down

muscle, fat, softening carrots,
potato skins loosening, leftovers
I'll eat on Sunday when I return.

This morning, I bet my wife
pulled the sheets and
bedspread extra tight

before tucking in the pillows
and scraped the lowboy clean
of my change and receipts

on her way to the shower.
And like you, Hopper's man,
I want to see something,

anything, but a bed
in the rectangle
of light before me,

my hand curled
into my inner thigh,
too, shirt tripped

open as I slump. I, too,
no longer feel the woman
beside me in bed, friend.

I, too, see the pages blank
in books I left open
the night before.

I, too, can't bear my foot
toeing into the light.

HAVING BUMMED A SMOKE OUTSIDE OF THE NATIONAL GALLERY, THOUGH I HAVE QUIT

> And if it rains, a closed car at four. And we shall play
> a game of chess.
> —ELIOT

The trees stick out
their tongues
at all of us squatting

at their trunks while wild onions
fall limp at their tips
like month-old mohawks.

Candy-coated tourist
buses park toe to heel.
Yesterday, sushi

and a slipped-off
boot and socked foot
in the lap for lunch

and noodles and beef alone
in Chinatown last night.
Will another woman ever

place her handbag on the grass,
commando-crawl to it, finger
the stalk-eye of her camera,

and snap twenty shots
of the Capitol dome
perched upon her slouched

purse like a Pope's mitre?
Would Cézanne study this team
of Segways rolling past

with their unmanned eyes
and over-ripened helmets?
Would Rousseau replace

the mannered Samoyed
with a jeweled collar and thin
leash and hook up

this albino squirrel
begging for a cheese danish
instead, stroking it wild

as the boy in a harness
pulling with all his strength
against his mother's thick strap,

the Washington Monument
distending from his hunched back;
Modigliani wouldn't have

to stretch the mother's face
beyond the long length
it has become.

The stoled woman
reckoning a Claesz
in the Gallery

asked no one out loud,
"Who would eat
a peacock pie,

all its feathers
in a vase beside it?"
"And all of those blue eyes

flirting with you,"
I responded,
"and I would."

WHEN PUBIC BECOMES PUBLIC

—Tom Wesselmann's *Great American Nude #57*

Daffodil demi-bob,
satsuma bedpost,

pouty curtains—
and he dipped
from the same arch

of his palette
for her vulcanized

nipples that he did
for the crevice
of her mouth.

The beach and ocean
nuzzle one another
out the window.

Black stars behave
within the angle iron

of her *Oh-My* arm.
The cheetah chaise longue
beneath her

ripples its pattern
of runes, vertebrae,

knuckles, shark teeth.
A parched veldt
of public hair erupts.

HOLES AND FOLDS

—Jean Honoré Fragonard's *The Swing*

The lions lounge
without hunger
in this landscape,

skeeting spring water
into marble spittoons.

But what will the lady
in the just-opened iris
dress see after the swing

reaches its full forward arc
and the taut rope

sends the iris blind
into the canopy's hole,
branches pressing

broken fingers and limp wrists
upon soil where green refuses

to grow? Her six young friends
before her repose on the grass
in an egg of sunlight,

their torsos jutting
like a limestone outcropping.

Can the woman
in the same iris dress
behind the six sycophants,

her petals wilting over the edge
of the crypt she teeters on,

see her younger, more beautiful
sister's fate in the long spyglass
she aims like a musket just beyond

her sister's arm, a rifle itself
sighting in the sun bent

behind a storm cloud,
or has her lover's arm slipping
along her mother's grave

already reached too far
into the folds of her dress?

BACK TO THE OLD CITY

—A. Thomas Schomberg's *Rocky*

How cordial,
the cars

and delivery
trucks rounding
the fountains

and bronzes,
the patina teal

as it should be,
fine mist of rain,
barely perceptible,

hawk circling
the stairs

where children raise
their arms
in victory.

And all
of the men

cheeked
in the remnants
of their vainglory

gather around
Rocky's knees,

fists balled
above their heads.
They will not

run up the stairs,
or will I,

middle age
and untenable shoes
the likenesses

we shun but share.
The buses exhaust

themselves on the curb,
noses sliming
the windows like slugs.

Only a few pass the tents
set up for a beer tasting

to enter the museum.
The rest open
their umbrellas,

garish perennials
blooming too early,

and find their way,
partly convinced
of their greatness,

into the old city
staged across the sky

before us, the faint
cries of "Yo, Adrian!"
unlike birdsong, behind.

FOUR MOVES TO THE FOCAL POINT

—Balthus's *The Street*

His knee is too far
up the back
of her skirt.

His cheek scours
her ear, his hand

clutching her
entire forearm
as if it were a pipe wrench.

He says he will teach
her the bal musette,

his torso compressing
like an accordion
at "–ette," his voice pulsing

from bellow shake
to a sharp tremolo

when he says,
"*Je ne suis pas
si vieux.*"

MY VIEW FROM HERE

—Yves Tanguy's *Les Vues*

Like a man running away
from his tumor (legs fuzzy
with speed) skull contorting
to the cancer's protean form—
a bicuspid pliered from the roots,
enamel gone, dentin starting to slouch
like pudding—stages 2, 3
lurking on the desert floor
below him, stage 4
suspended behind him
like a vodka bottle
barked with decades of wax.

Like the cowboy last night
at the hotel bar who had
already drunk his way through
the top-shelf whiskey,
who asked if I fished
before I had slid halfway
onto the barstool,
like his unfettered cough
of a confession that these
were the first drinks
he had knocked back
in eight years,
like the biopsy results
he received earlier that day,
the hospital bed and gown
he refused, the surgery,
radiation, chemo ("lab rat shit")
he won't do, like the three
phone calls from MD Anderson,

his ring tone set to the *Jaws* theme,
while he talked about native cutthroat
and his girlfriend sat motionless,
her eyes full of agency at first
then dropped to the overwrought
fried green tomatoes
she wouldn't touch.

Like my best friend
and fishing buddy of forty years
in his last hour of gurgling,
his final movements trying
to wipe away his piss as if some
primitive reflex awakened by dignity.

Like a bass lumbering in deep water
at his pond during winter,
like his patience, twitching a jig
all day in hope of one big bite.

Like the glioblastoma the cowboy
and my best friend shared, the food
they could no longer taste, the splinters
in their necks, the names
of their children lost in pill bottles,
like the *me* I see now
in *Les Vues,* the grey smudge
and outline of something
that they never catch up to
no matter how fast they run,
no matter how long I wait for them.

BLIND SPOT

—Warhol's *Rorschach*

Too easy
to say Shiva

or Janus
or butterfly
effect or tree

of life or
Christmas

wreath because
it is December
or hood ornament

or Pompeii
or ball mask

or Burgundy
masque or drop
zone or topo map

or gilded intestines,
Barneys, Wall Street.

Instead, please see
a honey *P*
inscribed inside

a Wonder
Bread fold-over.

THE APOSTLE

—Picasso's *Woman Playing with a Small Cat*

To lure it
from her finger
curls, she rips out

a tuft, dangles it
like a liver

lollipop—the cat
now at a lap revival

strikes a midair
hallelujah.

ASTRAL IMAGE AS ENSIGN

—Rothko's *Astral Image*

Make me your jelly,

the tumescence of seed

and gelatin, then boil

and reduce me, leave

me to cool. Peel off

the caramelized sheaf

of me from the pot's gut.

Carve out a pyramid

with my navel at its core,

my knot of lineal thread,

my dent of identity.

ICONOCLASTS

—Robert Indiana's *The American Dream #1*

Four boys dot the marble floor
beside Rauschenberg's *Rebus.*
The smallest draws a mosquito

with a bright red proboscis
as thick and long as his pen.

Another boy fills the loose leaf
with sprung Slinkys and tight
graphite curls. Before he can say what

his "mutant" is doing, the docent
corrects him: "No, not mutant—

think of a riddle, symbols whose names
sound like intended words." The boys
look at him as if they stepped in shit,

their skittery visions noodled from their guts
and field-dressed in the painting

now reduced by the docent
into the same thin sheet of gray.
So one boy looks left, takes out his finger,

and the rest turn and pull theirs out
and one-eye their sights at Indiana's

targets: first at the star labeled "Tilt"
then "Take All" then placing pistols
back in their holsters and shouldering rifles,

they dump banana clips and drum
magazines into "The American Dream."

TRAYMORE HOTEL: A STUDY IN FALSE CONSCIOUSNESS

—Artshwager's *Destruction III*

The penthouse suite
buckles like a racehorse's knee,

the herringbone stitching
from the fourteenth floor to lobby
busting loose from the first

few blasts. Drapes
loiter in windows.

The grand entrance
bloats with cauliflower curds.

The middle floors'
maw turns inside out,

exposing horns of plenty
which spill Chinese dragons,
heads down, nostrils flared.

Shards of black acrylic
linger on the Celotex

like flakes of dark chocolate
or razor-shaved truffles
or petals of coal,

NO ONE IS KNOCKING

—Ivan Albright's *Into the World There Came a Soul Called Ida*

Everything sags
eventually—

calves coming
to rest in doughy

pleats at the ankles,
the wicker chair's

fallen curls.
Even the bureau

leans downhill
(cigarette burned

back to the astragal
edge, the soiled

Q-tip, the slumped
dollar bills,

comb almost dipping
its weight

out of balance)
as if the earth

beneath the house
has had enough, too,

shrugs its shoulders,
lifting up one corner

of the bedroom
and opening a hole

in the other, dumping
Ida and all

she has left
in it. And she

sees it all
unfolding

behind her
in the hand

mirror and powder-
puffs, powder-puffs

the flush in her chest
that is no longer there.

CRANES ARCING LIKE STATIC

    —Bonnard's *Young Woman Writing*
    —For Dan O'Brien

Regrets, Thank Yous,
a thread of ink
suturing a lover's wound—

these notes laying
a flagstone path
across the red-velvet table.

I wish to see her knees,
her legs more stable
than the chair

she leans out of.
Or maybe these
are poems she will

fold into origami: cranes,
1,000 of them, Sadako,
for healing, 1,000 poems

for healing. But she
would not know
about Sadako.

Or maybe they
are blank, a subject bold
and ugly at the head,

pencil points dug in
at every left-hand corner
but not quite in the same spot,

which, if stacked and shuffled
like an old cartoon, would coalesce
and jump like static in a dark room.

BORDERS

—Hopper's *Cape Cod Evening*

But it seems
noonish, as if
a flash just burst
above a photographer's
shroud, except for the firs,
blue as parrotfish,
with night bulging
through their needles.
At first, the man
on the stoop, white

sleeves rolled to the empty
shot glass of his shoulder,
seems to look
beyond the frame,
following the dog's
eyes to some night sound,
but as I move closer,
he isn't. He follows
his hand into

the tall grass, the same
grass that swallows
his wife to her knees.
She folds her arms
at her waist, leaning
against their white
house with red trim
like an inverted
stop sign. She will not
talk tonight. He hasn't
talked for years.

TRISTESSE I: MATTRESS AS CANVAS

—Philip Guston's *Couple in Bed*

Always the soles
of work boots
and a table

of broken ankles,
soles cut
at the heel

like a leaner
cocked on a post—
another toss

shy of a ringer—
and even
in bed: sapling

tibias, soled
but unmanned,
resting on the top sheet

like mauls, Guston's
and his wife's heads
conjoined, bulging

like a single brain, but still
he squeezes the brush handles,
horsehair petalled,

angry with paint,
thumb cocked, hitching
a ride to his next canvas.

A STUDY OF INTERGROUP RECONCILIATION

—Nauman's *Eat/Death*, Gonzalez-Torres's *Untitled (Portrait
of Ross in L.A.)*, Warhol's *Twenty-Five Colored Marilyns*, and
Noland's *Bluewald*

On the fluorescent sign
I try to read as *DINER*,

EAT ripens orange
as coiled eyes
on a stove

inside the *D* and *H*
buttressing *DEATH*.

And piled beside it,
hard candy
like cabochon-

cut jewels
begs us to take

and eat this gift
and thus diminish
its ideal weight

of 175 pounds.
And we do—

first, the woman with rainbows
on her fleece socks
for three butterscotches.

Then a bald man fingers
a cinnamon round

and whispers a prayer
I am close enough to eat,
and I bow my head

and close my eyes with him.
We all eat and eat and eat

(the spicy, the sweet)
like what took the artist's love
from him and wait

for the replenished pile
his statement promises.

Twenty-five Marilyns nod and lip
from the next room, lemon hair
tunneling across her foreheads,

mint eye shadow
and collars still lingering

in the roofs of our mouths.
Oswald, paper-punched seven times,
his body reddening, would curse us as fools

of art if the Flag were not
stuffed into his mouth like a gag.

THE BLUFF

—Louis Lozowick's *Thanksgiving Dinner*

A stack
of bread
teeters

in a loose
shuffle like

a loaded deck
of cards. Iris
beards swell

from the pot
of soup. The man

with an ash-
tray chin and
pool-pocket

eyes suspends
his fist over

dinner like a sledge.
The other men
in line

aren't thankful
for him.

BREAKFAST AT THE MENIL

—Dali's *Eggs on the Plate Without the Plate*

Always time stretched to its limit,
the bezel unfazed, the hour

in a drip I would have flicked
out of impatience or boredom.

Sunnyside up I ordered this morning,
though at home I scramble.

The two eggs couple on Dali's plate,
the one overhead hanging like a head

of garlic, the yolk a window, a cross
subsumed by an empty box.

Ride the carrot sheath to the green tops
and scale the hole with me,

where a pappy and his grand
find yellow for the first time,

not the yolk, not a rain slicker,
but this yellow they see

in this moment with me
while breakfast goes chillingly cold.

MULIERCULA: HOMUNCULUS
AS DAUGHTER

—Pierre Bonnard's *Le Peignoir*

She sleeps
in her skin,
chin tucked

into her chest
like a pigeon

on a power line,
hair brushed
and brushed

then pinned.
My daughter

says, "mermaid,"
the woman's
chiffon flaring

with gold carp
scales, lily pads
floating above

her head like
empty thought

bubbles. Where
my daughter
sees a fish

tail, I plead
for rectrices,

a bit of down
beaked to the surface
and preened,

the signature
an ibis head.

When I say
the daisy petals

behind the bird-
woman prove

she is on land,
my daughter says,
"Silly Daddy,

those are ice
minnows

tickling her back
to wake her up
from a nap."

And at once,
water and air

are no longer
distinct elements
and pathways,

and I truly
understand

why one must
concede at times
even if one is right.

TRISTESSE II: MANIFEST DESTINY, LATE 20TH CENTURY

—Frank Moore's *Prairie*

Of course
snow falls
in the bedroom:

ice crystals
like raised bites.

Buffalos
the size
of bedbugs

migrate across
the comforter,

their violet
trailings
the only proof

that they
were really there.

CORTICAL AROUSAL

—Picasso's *Acrobat*

Discharge leg,
one hand

en pointe,
the other

a dislocated
fork. Sniff

own butt. Go
to the café:

bend backward
to impress!

NOT-STORY

—Rothko's *Street Scene*

Perhaps he still had crumbs
on his lips, his collar, his lap
when he unzipped. Perhaps

he was still bound in half-sleep,
looking back at his memory
pressed into the mattress.

Perhaps the streetlamp's inquisition
through the open window
persuaded the cracker-mattress

skyscraper to press its bald head
flat against the frame or the woman
horrified by its sight to boil

in her own skin, a red almost too orange,
crabs dumped across the Sunday news.
No one else is hungry or horny here.

The brown stripe of a man wedges
into a breezeway. A granddaughter,
her dress a swarm of chips clipped

from the thumb-moon, legs simmering
from ankle to shin to knee,
cooling to pink at the hemline,

her arm outstretched, elbowless,
impeding her grandmother's path.
Rothko said he was no colorist

and a painting is not an experience.
Don't be coy. Make me believe in this innocence
of nothing, the not-story of our lives.

OVERHEARD

—de Kooning's *Evacuation*

"You see the figures,
torsos, torsos?"

"Yeah, yeah, I guess so."

"Teeth, teeth, typical
de Kooning teeth."

"You can't give them back."

"A horrible head."

"Ah, that ruins it."

"The rice fields ruin it."

"Early Black Period—
one show, his breakthrough."

"See the crack?"

"Must be a board."

"And his late work goes back to that."

"Oh, look, a penis,
and that eye, a vagina."

"Rice fields, workers, right?"

SOCIAL CAPITAL AND THE INTRODUCTION
OF THE VANILLA EGG

—Kandinsky's *Small Pleasures* and *Yellow Cow*

A pile
of sheep
or armful

of balloons,
dribbling trail

of purses
opening
in unison,

unnecessary
cane, Dreamsicle

scarf corkscrewing
the neck,

but we distrust
Kandinsky's

pleasures
and the overpriced
café where

the tour ends
almost
as much

as each other,
our headphones

still cupping
our ears
for safety

from each other.
If I carved

with my pen the front
leg of *Yellow Cow*
for brisket would

security let me be?
Would everyone

unplug, order the blue ribs,
the black hooves
halved from me?

And after we partook,
who would divide

the vanilla egg
beneath her udder
so we could share,

all of us share,
something sweet?

ON THE HAY LEDGE

It's frozen motion; time is holding its breath for an
instant—and for eternity. That's what I'm after.
—ANDREW WYETH

Wheat straw
piles beneath me

clapboard's
furrowed grain

swirls into imperfection
seed corn hangs

in the balance
of rafters

like birds
caught in a snare

feed bucket
brims with moonlight

shadows
spill over the side

SCHOLARS' ADVICE

—Rothko's *Untitled (Seagram Mural Sketch)*

The scholars warn:
Don't mistake it
for a whore's door

or heaven's lore
for the poor,
or, God forbid,

boorish spores or s'mores
(context, imposition,
Children!) or a pompadour—

orange paint weeping
from its wick—or
existential gore!

Or a haphazard pour
of caution cone or
windows scored

by a soothsayer
drunk or eyes
pied, squared,

then cored or
sores of an invalid
left to flounder

on the tile floor,
which, in my ramblings
here, I find my father,

cord pulled while
on the pot, embolism,
a few minutes, and gone.

A hole within a hole
of the whole, a thought
without thought, they

would want me to see.
Pander to my drama
and despair, scholars.

My mind fancies to open the door
and to lie on the floor
where my father was no more.

ANTIPOSITIVISM

—Lichtenstein's *Brushstroke with Spatter*

A finger inches,
trying to count
the Ben-Day dots

speckling the backdrop
like chiggers dug into
spread lats, then gives up

to Google.
The black and yellow stripe
twists like a garter

snake or the fatwood
seeping turpentine
it muscled beneath.

The blue spatter defies
the arbitrary or unconscious,
its drips and bars and dashes

profiled in black
willful as lines in a coloring book:
a crab carapace thinning

to a tapeworm then swelling
to two lovers' enfettered torsos
keeping traction on a horse skull.

Then another finger,
trying to count
the Ben-Day dots.

LOOKING-GLASS SELF

—John Sloan's *Clown Making Up*

He's sugar
glass,

a birdbath
in the moonlight's

sudden freeze,
the lantern's

mantle—belly
of gas, hanging

like a pear
in the globe.

MEMORY AS BURNT FABRIC

—Picasso's *Woman Ironing*

Whose sheet or trousers
compelled her to bend over,

the contour of her back a clay hill,
the space between her arms
as she leans her weight into the iron

another torso, wisps of hair tangling
across her forehead into bass clefs?

Her dress is thin as ankle skin.
She has fallen asleep, the wedge
she holes into the fabric a week's pay.

MEMORY AS WOOD GRAINS

—Picasso's *The Blind Man's Meal*

He measures the jug's
crackle glaze in fingertips, slides
his thumb across the dinner roll

as if it were the back
of a lover's hand.

The bowl once bellied
with balsamic and olive oil.

The alder tabletop
no longer knows its age,

the blind man's elbows
now burling and fiddlebacking
their own history into the grain.

WHEN THE ELEPHANT LEAVES THE ROOM

—Magritte's La Chambre d'ecoute

Untusk the elephant!
Tickle the peanuts
from its trunk;

grab its riding-crop tail,
and back it out
of the room.

Roll in apple! Green,
two weeks from ripe.
Slide into a wingback

and wait for Mrs. Repondre
to say, "The tea cups
are a bit pedestrian

for the scones, don't you think?"
Watch the apple swell,
juice filling the scars

in the oak floor. The host
tries to nudge the apple
under the punch table,

but it is already too large.
Watch it swell and swell,
green stretching its limits

and splintering into tertiaries,
the guests becoming louder
and louder in willful ignorance.

Watch the crown moulding
accept the shadows of the stem,
the people now skirting

the room's edges
like camel crickets, their voices
pressing into a single note,

a single reverberation
just below the summit of F.
Listen to the apple in the room.

MIMESCAPE

—Robert Longo's *Pressure*

If I
were a mime
in despair,

I, too,
would wear

the cityscape
and mercury

sky as a paper
hat and Band-Aid
walls as an undershirt.

SENTENCE

—Andrew Wyeth's *Christina's World*

She awoke
to an empty house,

the corn crib hollow,
ladder to the roof
untended, the tire tracks

ending at the house
the sentence

she can't quite finish.
So she crawled
into the field

like a skink to sun,
her legs dragging

behind her like a tail.
She is pink
in the dying grass.

THEODICY

—Bellows's *Massacre at Dinant* and *The Germans Arrive*

The clergy raise
their gooseneck
arms to the God

who wouldn't soften
the steel of bayonets
while the dust clouds

from German boots
through the next town
piggyback the countryside.

The butcher holds his wife
to his chest like a side of beef
while an old woman

pitchforks her hands,
her husband lacing his
into a blindfold.

The couple on the floor
next to me splice
their fingers

in loose knots,
arms contracting
and dilating like mouths

after climax
or before death.
On the canvas

above the couple's mingling,
the Belgian boy's severed
hand hitchhikes

on the ground
that could be
a threshing floor,

centuries-old
grain lodged in the cracks
like mortar joints,

while a German soldier
nooses him with an elbow.
The smoke heaves

and purls from rooftops
like David dancing
in a rage after Uzzah

laid hands on the jostled Ark
and God smote him
for David's sin.

NOON MASS AT SACRÉ COEUR

"Chut, s'il vous plaît,"
the nun says,
her mouth

stretching
to the starched
wimple

that etches
the bones
of her face:

"chut, chut—mass."
Another tourist
dips his sweaty hand

into the marble stoup,
flicking holy water
toward his son.

Townspeople slip
through the visitors
to the nave—

some with pressed shirts,
thin dresses covered
with flour.

When the nineteen-ton
Savoyarde Bell
silences the streets,

the altar boys lean
toward the sacristy.
The priest stands,

chanting French and Latin.
The celebrants line up
beneath the mosaic

of Joan of Arc
and St. Michael
fawning over

Christ's hands:
this morning,
I saw these saints'

adoring looks
shine on the faces
of the Three Shades

of Death in Rodin's
Gates of Hell.
Admiring their fists,

the brothers offer gifts
for the damned
drowning in their sins.

As I stand behind
a velvet rope,
the priest raises the cup,

offers it hand to hand,
its polished sides reflecting
their disciplined lips.

AT ROTHKO CHAPEL

—in memory of Mark Strand

All silent prayers

in the confusion

and negative

    space

    absence

what is not

    and what is

poker

    late one night

clubs and spades

    black

and presence

and I see you

of positive

with you

in white

suspended

you caught in a bluff

"nothing"

                    of you

                              down your cheeks

                                        persnickety simplicity

                    what was left

                                        for absence

as if bestowing us

                    of the creases

                    somehow fitting   your

dark purple lines   it embodies

     at the centers   making things whole

a sip of red wine
     red Italian glasses
          matching red socks

like a paper clip made tool   by a crow
the biscuit hole   in a sheet of dough
          one the vehicle
          absence so aware

the other

you said   almost

both

RE-STROKE I

—Balthus's *Nude Before a Mirror*

The perennials must be on fire
outside, the dahlias, jonquils.

The lavender water pitcher
must have been an afterthought,
its somewhat existence

not even worth a reflection:
I want her to snap off its handle

and slip it over her veiny wrist
like a Bakelite bracelet.
I want to re-stroke the canvas,

harden that afterthought
and place it in her hands

so she can toss it out
the open window
where Balthus crouches.

RE-STROKE II

—Artschwager's *In the Driver's Seat*

The pointy man next to me
says, "Ah, to be
that skinny!" And I say,

"Yes, we are plump!" "Speak
for yourself," he responds

and skinnies off to *Door II.*
And I wonder if I should have said,
"And, ah, to be that naked!"

So I name the naked guy
on the beach pretending

to be in the cockpit
of a dragster "Skinny"
and the pointy man "Cock."

THE KISS

—Matisse's *Studio, Quai Saint-Michel*

Canvas within
a canvas.

He stepped
back

from his chair
and easel,

thus reducing
her,

leaving the hip
and thigh

charcoaled
close enough

to twirl
her hair

at the kiss
of her elbow.

The ink pot
clutches the table.

Beside me,
on the museum bench,

a baby screams,
the mother

shooing and cooing
the infant

then plopping
out a breast.

Even the mother
shudders at first.

FISTING THE TINE

—Homer's *Girl with Pitchfork*

Her blood orchid
index finger curls
to her thumb

in an *OK*
at the crux
of the pitchfork,

but nothing
seems OK,
harbor wind

lifting her dress
in a catawampus
teepee, haystack

a windowless hut,
lighthouse
centipeding

to the fir line.
She will not
pitch the hay

today, the sky
too eerily clear
in Homer's

overshadowed
field. To the man
pushing his glasses

down to read
the brass placard,
the pitchfork

is a wishbone.
He reaches out
and pulls down

on the tine: "Big end
is mine," he says
to me, "but I have

no more wishes"
and pretends
to toss it over

his shoulder
as he side-steps
to the typical

Homer. But
the girl
in the hayfield

would reach down
if she could, unclasp
her *OK,* fist the tine,

cut a door
into the nearest bale,
wish herself inside.

WHAT IS NOT FLESH COMES TO A POINT

—Rothko's *Phalanx of the Mind*

Everything is a weapon
   the glass pane poised
      in the geometry
of its shanks
   even the shadows
      when imposed
by the brain's
   peach-pit wrinkles
      onto what
could be

floor   ceiling   sky

and all

with the same
   sharp intent

thin   impaled   desire

like an acupuncturist's needle
   a parabola of musings above
      a flaccid tongue
         and its balmy shadow below
            massaging the pane to shatter
              into the not-flesh of us all

RE-STROKE III: STILL LIFE
WITH BANYAN TREE

—Buenos Aires

A wreck
of elephants

that took root:
the homeless

settle inside
channels

of its dugout
canoes

lined with
faded drapes.

The dog sitter's
body

sickles against
his leash

of horny mutts.
Pigeons blink

amber oil
and bone.

Three girls
with heels

and skirts
too high

and hyacinths
blinking from

their crowbar
waists

ring-a-round
a lamppost,

its steepled
hat aslant,

a drunken
clown.

And I
the watcher

am being
watched.

My arm
drapes

across
a cankled root,

my heels
fused, knees

spread,
void between

like a dugout
canoe:

the cardboard
sketch the man

with blinking eyes
hands me.

And in return,
I rip out

the poem
this one was.

We even
trade.

He slips
into

his banyan tree's
dugout canoe.

I uncap
my pen

and turn
the page.

CPSIA information can be obtained
at www.ICGtesting.com
Printed in the USA
LVOW03s1806220218
567566LV00002B/307/P